WORLD IN FOCUS

FOCUS ON
Indonesia

SALLY MORGAN

WORLD ALMANAC® LIBRARY

Please visit our web site at: www.garethstevens.com
For a free color catalog describing World Almanac® Library's list of high-quality books
and multimedia programs, call 1-800-848-2928 (USA) or 1-800-387-3178 (Canada).

ISBN 978-0-8368-6750-3 (lib. bdg.)
ISBN 978-0-8368-6757-2 (softcover)

This North American edition first published in 2008 by
World Almanac® Library
A Weekly Reader Corporation imprint
200 First Stamford Place
Stamford, CT 06912 USA

Commissioning editor: Nicola Edwards
Editor: Patience Coster
Inside design: Chris Halls, www.mindseyedesign.co.uk
Cover design: Wayland
Series concept and project management by EASI-Educational Resourcing
(info@easi-er.co.uk)
Statistical research: Anna Bowden
Maps and graphs: Martin Darlison, Encompass Graphics

World Almanac® Library editor: Alan Wachtel
World Almanac® Library cover design: Scott M. Krall

Picture acknowledgments. The author and publisher would like to thank the following for allowing their pictures to be reproduced
in this publication:
Alamy 43 (Vince Bevan); CORBIS 4 (Nik Wheeler), 5 (Anders Ryman), 6 (Beawiharta/Reuters), 8 (WEDA/epa), 9 (Stapleton Collection),
10, 11 (Bettmann), 12 (Crack Palinggi/Reuters), 13 (Reuters), 16 (Stephen Frink), 17 (Owen Franken), 18 (Wolfgang Kaehler), 19 (Sergio
Dorantes), 22 (Kevin Lamarque/Reuters), 23 (Bagus Indahono/epa), 24 (Beawiharta/Reuters), 25 (Jacqueline M. Koch), 27 (Justin Guariglia),
28 (Wolfgang Kaehler), 30 (Supri/Reuters), 31 (Tarmizy Harva/Reuters), 32 (Supri/Reuters), 33 (Crack Palinggi/ Reuters), 34
(POOL/Reuters), 35 (Reuters), 36 (Reuters), 37 (Lirio Da Fonseca/Reuters), 38 (James Robert Fuller), 39 (Beawiharta/Reuters), 41
(Kaveh Kazemi), 42 (Tarmizy Harva/Reuters), 44 (Crack Palinggi/Reuters), 45 (Lindsay Hebberd), 46 and *title page* (Mast Irham/epa),
47 (Free Agents Limited), 48 (Barry Lewis), 49 (Supri/Reuters), 51 (Reuters), 52 (Stuart Westmorland), 53 (Stuart Westmorland),
54 (Wolfgang Kaehler), 56 (Mast Irham/epa), 57 (Robert Harding World Imagery), 59 (Tarmizy Harva/Reuters); CORBIS Sygma 26
(Jufri Kemal); EASI-Images/Simon Scoones 14, 15; EASI-Images/Ed Parker 20, 29, 55; EASI-Images/Clive Sanders 21; EASI-Images/
Jenny Matthews 40, 58; EASI-Images/Neal Cavalier-Smith 50.

The directional arrow portrayed on the map on page 7 provides only an approximation of north.
The data used to produce the graphics and data panels in this title were the latest available at the time of production.

Printed in China

1 2 3 4 5 6 7 8 9 10 09 08 07

CONTENTS

Cover and Title page: In Denpasar, Bali, dancers wearing elaborate headdresses take part in the Melasti ceremony, in which the victory of good over evil is celebrated.

CHAPTER 1

Indonesia – An Overview

Indonesia is the largest archipelago in the world. It is made up of 17,508 islands. The Indonesian archipelago extends for more than 3,107 miles (5,000 km) between the Asian and Australian mainlands. Indonesia is the world's fourth most populous country after China, India, and the United States. In 2006, Indonesia had over 245 million people living in an area of 705,006 square miles (1,826,440 square kilometers), which is almost three times the size of Texas. Strategically, Indonesia is one of the most important nations in Southeast Asia, because it is positioned at the crossroads between the continents of of Asia and Australia and between the Indian and Pacific Oceans. One of the most important sea routes in the world—a narrow stretch of water called the Straits of Malacca—lies between Sumatra, the westernmost island of Indonesia, and Malaysia. More than 50,000 vessels pass through the Straits of Malacca each year, carrying up to one-quarter of the world's sea trade, including oil for China and Japan.

A DIVERSE NATION

Millions of years ago, a land bridge existed between the Indonesian islands and Asia. Early humans could walk between one and the other. One million years ago, the sea level rose and cut Indonesia off from the mainland. This separation did not stop people from reaching the islands.

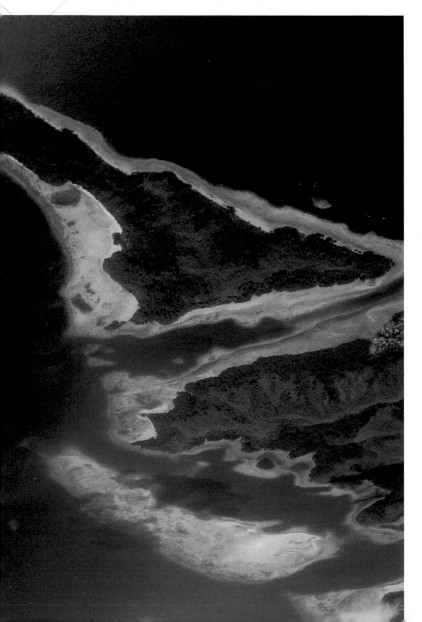

◄ Indonesia's thousands of islands give the country a long and varied coastline with many sandy beaches, rugged cliffs, and forests that run down to the sea.

During the last few thousand years, immigrant peoples have traveled to Indonesia by boat from Malaysia, Thailand, and Vietnam and from Melanesia in the east, bringing with them their cultures and languages.

Indonesia's national motto is "Unity in Diversity." This motto reflects the fact that the country's population is made up of more than 300 ethnic groups, each with its own language and culture. These diverse groups are drawn together by their common language, Bahasa Indonesia, which is spoken throughout the islands. Although Indonesia's great diversity has enriched the culture, it has made governing the country very difficult.

Between 1623 and 1942, Indonesia was controlled by the Dutch. Japan invaded in 1942

▲ In June 2000 on the island of Bali, members of a local Hindu temple carry out a purification rite on the beach. Women carry sacred objects on their heads as part of the temple's anniversary celebrations.

and remained until 1945. The Dutch returned in 1945. For the next four years, there were hostilities between the Dutch and the Indonesians. Indonesia finally gained its independence in 1949. Governing Indonesia has not been straightforward. Successive governments have had problems such as corruption, human rights abuses, and poverty.

? Did You Know?

The name Indonesia has its roots in two Greek words: "Indos," meaning "Indian," and "Nesos," which means "islands."

◀ In the early morning on a busy street in Indonesia's capital, Jakarta, a young boy sleeps on the pavement while people go about their daily business. Despite government programs to fight poverty, homelessness is still a problem in Indonesia's major cities.

Ethnic unrest in the provinces of Aceh (at the northern tip of Sumatra), Papua, and East Timor (both islands in the country's far east) has made Indonesia's recent history bloody.

The country has recently emerged from four decades of authoritarianism during which the military was powerful, free speech was restricted, and human rights were not respected. Today, it has a democratically elected president and a government that is beginning to implement reforms. The challenges confronting Indonesia include corruption, widespread poverty, ethnic unrest, demands for more self-rule, and the fight against terrorism.

Did You Know?

The red bar on the Indonesian flag symbolizes human blood and bravery, and the white bar represents the human spirit, peace, and honesty. The colors and design are based on the flag used by the once powerful Hindu Majapahit Empire, which ruled Java (the main island of the Indonesian archipelago) during the thirteenth century. The Majapahit Empire flag had nine red and white stripes.

Physical Geography

- Land area: 705,006 sq miles/ 1,826,440 sq km
- Water area: 35,898 sq miles/93,000 sq km
- Total area: 740,904 sq miles/ 1,919,440 sq km
- World rank (by area): 17
- Land boundaries: 1,759 miles/2,830 km
- Border countries: East Timor, Malaysia, Papua New Guinea
- Coastline: 34,000 miles/54,716 km
- Highest point: Puncak Jaya (16,503 ft/5,030 m)
- Lowest point: Indian Ocean (0 ft/0 m)

Source: CIA World Factbook

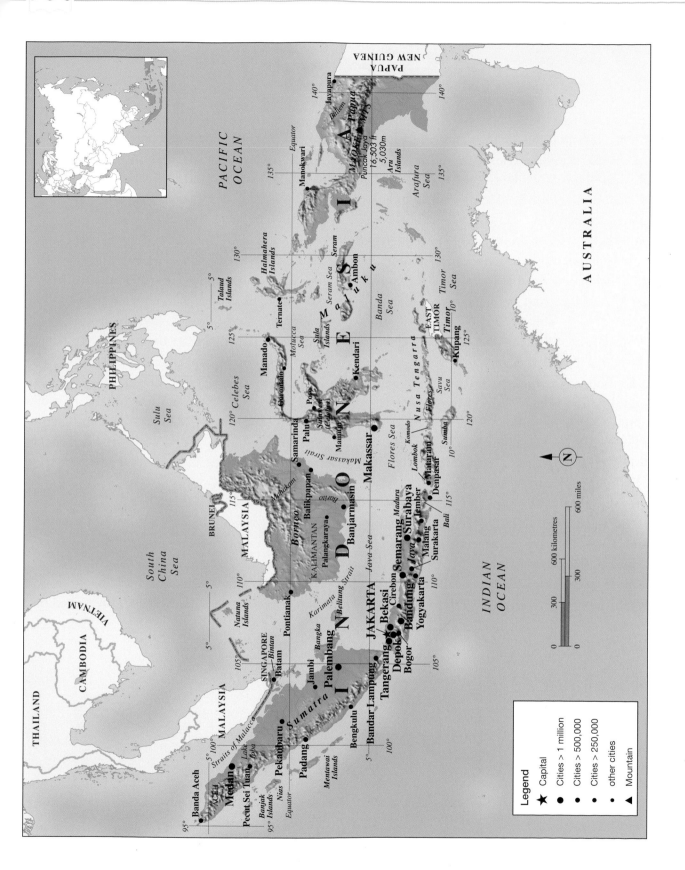

Legend

★ Capital
● Cities > 1 million
● Cities > 500,000
• Cities > 250,000
· other cities
▲ Mountain

CHAPTER 2

History

The history of the Indonesian islands stretches back 1.6 million years. Scientists have discovered fossils of a human ancestor, Java Man (*Homo erectus*), who lived in the east of Java (a major Indonesian island) at that time. Several thousand years ago, people moved into the region from islands to the east. Ever since that time, migrants have arrived in Indonesia from India, the Middle East, and Europe.

THE BUDDHIST AND HINDU KINGDOMS

Two thousand years ago, Indian traders and Buddhist and Hindu monks arrived in the islands. By the seventh and eighth centuries, a number of regions in Sumatra and Java were ruled by local kings who had adopted the Hindu or Buddhist faiths. These kings introduced Indian culture and customs to Indonesia, including Indian architecture, music, and dance. Between the seventh and thirteenth centuries, Sumatra was the center of an important Buddhist kingdom called Sri Vijaya. By the end of the thirteenth century, power had shifted from Sumatra to Java, where the Hindu kingdom of Majapahit was powerful. For the next two hundred years, the Majapahit Empire ruled over much of Indonesia and present-day Malaysia.

THE ARRIVAL OF ISLAM

During the fourteenth and fifteenth centuries, Muslim Arab traders arrived from North Africa and the Middle East via Malacca, an important trading center on mainland Malaysia. Gradually, the Majapahits retreated to Bali, a small island to the east of Java. By the sixteenth century, Java and Sumatra had become part of a Muslim empire with Islam as the main religion. The former Hindu kingdoms were divided into smaller Islamic states.

EUROPEAN TRADERS

As far as we know, the first European person to visit Indonesia was the Italian explorer Marco Polo, who landed by ship in Sumatra in about 1292. Other European traders followed, searching for spices that were highly prized in

► The Borobodur Temple dates back to the ninth century and is the largest Buddhist monument in Southeast Asia. Buddhist monks gather here to celebrate Vesakh Day, the most important day on the Buddhist calendar.

◀ This illustration shows French explorers on a "round-the-world" voyage at a boatyard near Kupang on the island of Timor in about 1820.

Europe. The Portuguese set up trading centers in the Maluku islands in northeast Indonesia in the early sixteenth century. The Dutch followed in 1596, and the English arrived in 1600.

The Europeans were soon fighting one another over the valuable spice trade. By 1623, the Dutch had emerged as the most powerful group, and they forced the Portuguese to retreat to East Timor and the English to retreat to other parts of Southeast Asia.

DUTCH RULE

Over the next 170 years, the Dutch East India Company extended its control over the islands. The local people tried unsuccessfully to force the Dutch out. In 1740, Chinese traders and local Indonesians started a rebellion in Jakarta, but it was quashed by the Dutch, who killed thousands of Chinese people. In 1799, the Dutch government seized control, and the region became known as the Dutch East Indies. The island of Bali remained

independent until 1906, when Dutch soldiers invaded and killed thousands of Balinese people.

THE NOVEMBER PROMISE

In 1918, the Dutch promised to grant self-government to the Indonesians in what was known as the "November promise." The promise was never fulfilled. As a compromise, the Dutch set up a body called the Volksraad, which was supposed to give more self-rule to the people, but it was powerless. By 1923, there was great unrest among the Indonesian people.

Did You Know?

In 2004, a previously unknown species of human called *Homo floresiensis* was discovered in a limestone cave on the Indonesian island of Flores. The 18,000-year-old skeleton was that of an adult just 3.28 feet (1 meter) tall. It is thought that *Homo floresiensis* reached Flores using bamboo rafts and may have lived in remote areas until a few thousand years ago.

In the 1920s, the financial problems of the United States and Europe had spread to Indonesia, and people went on strike in protest of rising levels of unemployment and poverty. The Dutch colonial government responded by censoring newspapers and restricting the freedom of the people, preventing them from gathering in public places. In July 1927, the Parti Nasional Indonesia (Indonesian Nationalist Party), or PNI, was formed. It was a militant group that refused to cooperate with the Dutch colonial government. The Dutch responded by putting some of the PNI leaders, including Achmed Sukarno and Muhammad Hatta, in jail.

An opportunity for change came during World War II. In 1942, Japan invaded the Dutch East Indies, and Sukarno and Hatta were released from jail. But it soon became clear that Japan was not prepared to give the Indonesians their independence; it wanted to rule the islands. The Indonesian people started to undermine Japanese control by attacking Japan's supply lines and garrisons. Finally, Japan allowed the Indonesian people to carry out much of their country's administration.

INDEPENDENCE

The end of World War II in the Pacific came in August 1945, when Japan's army surrendered to the Allies. Immediately, Sukarno and Hatta declared Indonesia an independent republic. Their triumph was short-lived. Within days, Dutch troops landed to reclaim power. The Indonesians resisted, and for the next four years, there was heavy fighting between the two sides. Finally, in November 1949, the United Nations (UN) managed to get the opposing sides to agree to Indonesian independence. A new constitution was drawn up, Sukarno was elected president, and Hatta became prime minister.

SUKARNO'S RULE

Sukarno had managed what seemed impossible—the unification of a very diverse group of people under one government and one language (Bahasa Indonesia). But his government was inefficient, and there was widespread corruption and administrative chaos. During the late 1950s, Sukarno expelled many Dutch colonists and claimed their property. The Dutch colonists controlled many of the businesses and owned much of the land,

► In 1944, during World War II, U.S. forces landed along the northern coast of Dutch New Guinea. In this picture, amphibious tanks have come ashore at Cape Sansapor.

► President Sukarno speaks to an angry crowd in Jakarta on October 17, 1952. The demonstration at which he was speaking was organized by senior members of the military who wanted to give Sukarno a reason to dissolve parliament. He refused, and in the months that followed, he replaced senior army officers with men more likely to do what he wanted.

so their departure severely disrupted the country's economy. Unemployment rose, and the population suffered great economic hardship. In 1958, the people of Sumatra rebelled, demanding more independence. The unrest spread to Sulawesi and other islands. Sukarno used the army to put down the rebellion, and his rule became stronger and more authoritarian. In 1960, he dissolved parliament and took control of the country. This marked the beginning of Sukarno's rule without a democratically elected government. At the same time, the Communist Party was growing in popularity; soon the two most powerful groups in Indonesia were the army and the Communist Party.

Focus on: East Timor

The province of East Timor gained independence from the Portuguese in 1975, but it was immediately taken over by Indonesia. Indonesia's takeover was not recognized by the United Nations. In the following years, separatists of the mostly Roman Catholic province resisted Indonesia's control. Indonesian troops moved in, and there was loss of life on both sides. The United States and human rights organizations voiced criticism of Indonesia's abuse of indigenous people in East Timor. In 1999, Indonesia reluctantly agreed to a referendum in which the East Timorese people could choose between limited self-rule within Indonesia and independence. They chose independence. This result triggered months of violence, during which Indonesia's army and armed militias carried out a campaign of terror against East Timor's people. The fighting forced thousands of people to flee their homes. The United Nations sent in a peacekeeping force to take over. In 2002, East Timor finally became independent.

THE FALL OF SUKARNO

In September 1965, the Communist Party tried to weaken the power of the army by assassinating six high-ranking officers. There was violence in the country's streets as students demonstrated against the communists. In the months that followed, many alleged communists were killed, including thousands of Indonesian Chinese. In 1966, Sukarno gave General Suharto supreme authority to bring the country to order.

THE SUHARTO ERA

Once order had been resumed, Suharto banned the Communist Party and appointed a new government with himself as chief executive. In 1967, Sukarno was voted out of power, and Suharto became president. He was reelected in 1973, 1978, 1983, 1988, 1993, and again in 1998. In these elections, however, Suharto was the only candidate. Although he improved the economy of the country, he ruled with an iron fist. Opposition parties were prevented from having a voice and government corruption grew worse. Suharto's downfall eventually came in 1997, when Indonesia's currency had to be devalued during the Asian Currency Crisis. This unstable situation led to riots as inflation and unemployment soared, and there was an outcry for Suharto to resign. Although he was reelected in 1998, Suharto resigned almost immediately. He was replaced by Vice President B. J. Habibie.

In 1999, Abdurrahman Wahid became the president of Indonesia. Wahid had campaigned on a pledge to fight corruption, but a few years later corruption scandals forced him to step down. In 2001, Megawati Sukarnoputri—Sukarno's daughter—was elected president. During her presidency, Indonesia's government granted limited self-rule to the provinces of Aceh and Papua. It was hoped that this would end the fighting in these regions, but it did not. Peace talks in Aceh failed and the army moved in again in 2003.

▶ President Megawati Sukarnoputri came to power in 2001. She is shown here visiting the Jakarta Stock Exchange in April 2004, just days before she was defeated in the general election.

Corruption was also a problem in Megawati Sukarnoputri's government. She was defeated in an election in 2004 by Susilo Bambang Yudhoyono. The election in which Yudhoyono became president was the first election in which Indonesians elected a president directly. Previously, the country's president was elected indirectly, by the legislature.

Focus on: The Troubled Province of Aceh

Although the people of the province of Aceh, in north Sumatra, are Muslims, their culture is different from the rest of Indonesia. Since 1976, separatists of the Free Aceh Movement have fought a campaign for independence. During this time, Indonesia's government has been unwilling to give the province independence because it wants to retain possession of Aceh's rich natural resources. In 2003, government troops moved in to crush the rebels. The fighting between the two sides continued until 2005. On December 26, 2004, an earthquake off the coast of Sumatra created a tsunami (tidal wave) that devastated Aceh, killing about 130,000 people and making half a million people homeless. The tsunami was the trigger for more peace talks and, in August 2005, Acehnese rebels and Indonesia's government signed a peace agreement to end the violence. The rebels agreed to disarm and stop their campaign for independence in exchange for more self-rule. Aceh is not the only province to have called for more independence. Uprisings have also occurred in Kalimantan (part of the island of Borneo) and Papua.

► In August 2002, Indonesian soldiers leave the province of Aceh after completing a three-month-long tour of duty. Beginning in 1976, thousands of Indonesian soldiers were sent to the region to fight the separatists. Thousands of people lost their lives on both sides of the conflict.

CHAPTER 3

Landscape and Climate

Indonesia is a nation of many islands, of which about 6,000 are inhabited. The country's largest islands are Java, Sumatra, and Sulawesi. Some of its major provinces are on islands that only partly belong to the country, such as Kalimantan (which makes up 60 percent of the island of Borneo) and Papua (part of the island of New Guinea). Papua was formerly a Dutch colony, but it was invaded by Indonesia in 1962 and has been controlled by Indonesia ever since. Many of Indonesia's islands have mountainous interiors surrounded by coastal plains. Its highest point is Mount Puncak Jaya in Papua, at 16,503 feet (5,030 m).

VOLCANIC ACTIVITY

Indonesia forms part of the "Ring of Fire," a vast circle of volcanoes located around the edge of the Pacific Ocean. There are more than 400 volcanoes in Indonesia, of which 130 are active. Most of them lie in a chain stretching from northern Sumatra through the islands of Java, Bali, Lombok, and Flores. About 70 of these volcanoes have erupted during the past 500 years. Mount Merapi, near Yogyakarta, is considered to be the most violent of the active volcanoes. It last erupted in June 2006.

Indonesia lies in an earthquake zone, and many areas experience minor tremors. The tsunami of December 2004 was the result of an underwater earthquake that caused violent movements in the ocean and created a huge tidal wave. On March 28, 2005, the island of Nias was hit by the second most powerful earthquake since 1965 and twelfth most powerful ever recorded. At least 800 people were killed and hundreds of buildings destroyed. An earthquake caused another tsunami on Java in July 2006.

◄ Mount Bromo is an active volcano that lies east in the province of Java. Its last major eruption was in 1966, but it had minor eruption in 2004.

THREE REGIONS

Geographically, Indonesia can be divided into three regions: the Sunda Shelf, the Sahul Shelf, and the Lesser Sundas. The Sunda Shelf includes the islands of Java, Madura, Sumatra, and Borneo, which are surrounded by shallow

▲ Many of the hillsides on the island of Bali are terraced and used as rice paddies. Terracing helps to reduce the amount of soil that is washed off the hillsides during heavy rainstorms.

seas. It extends from Malaysia to Thailand, Vietnam, and Cambodia. About 20,000 years ago, a land bridge joined these islands to the mainland of Asia, so the two regions have some types of plants and animals in common.

The province of Papua lies in New Guinea and, together with the nearby Aru islands, forms part of the Sahul Shelf. This region stretches south to the Australian coast. The Lesser Sundas are a group of islands that separate the Sunda and Sahul shelves. They include Maluku and Sulawesi and the islands of Nusa Tanggara. In this area, the surrounding seas are up to 16,404 feet (5,000 m) deep. This indicates that these islands were never joined to another land mass.

Focus on: Krakatoa

In 1883, a volcanic eruption on the island of Krakatoa was so violent that it blew the island apart. The eruption was five times more forceful than the explosion caused by the atomic bomb that was dropped on the city of Hiroshima, Japan, in 1945. It was heard thousands of miles away. The eruption created a tsunami that destroyed more than 160 villages along the coasts of Java and Sumatra and killed about 36,000 people. Ash and lava poured out of the volcano in such huge quantities that these deposits formed new islands.

RIVERS AND LAKES

Most Indonesian people live near water, either on a coast or by rivers and lakes. The country's largest rivers, including the Mahakam, Martapura, and Barito, are on Kalimantan, and they provide important routes to and from the mountainous interior. Papua has about 30 major rivers, most of which rise in the Maoke and Jayawijaya Mountains; these include the 249-mile- (400-km-) long Baliem River.

The largest lake in Indonesia is Lake Toba, in Sumatra. It covers 442 sq miles (1,145 sq km) and is surrounded by steep mountain cliffs. Lake Tempe in Sulawesi is also large but is shrinking fast because of the build-up of silt from soil erosion in the surrounding area. Some parts of the lake are less than 6.6 feet (2 m) deep and dry up completely during the dry season.

▲ The warm, clear seas that surround many of Indonesia's island provide perfect conditions for coral reefs. The reefs support a rich fish population, which is an important source of food for the local people. This reef is located near Sulawesi.

CLIMATE

Indonesia straddles the Equator, which means that it has a tropical climate. Its coastal plains are hot and humid all year round, with an average temperature of 82°F (28°C). The climate is cooler inland, where temperatures average about 79°F (26°C). It is cooler still in the higher mountain regions, where temperatures average about 73°F (23°C).

Indonesia has a monsoon climate, which includes a wet season followed by a dry season. Most parts of the country experience their wet season between November and March, when the winds blow from the northwest. Rain begins at about noon each day and lasts for a few hours. The dry season lasts from about June to October, when the winds blow from the south and east. Some areas, such as Maluku, have their wet season from March to August.

The lowland rainfall ranges between 70 inches and 126 inches (1,700 millimeters and 3,200 mm) per year, while mountain rainfall can reach 240 inches (6,100 mm) a year. The highest rainfall occurs in the mountainous regions, such as west Sumatra, the interior of Kalimantan, inland Java, and parts of Papua and Sulawesi. In these areas, average rainfall call be 236 inches (6,000 mm) or more. In contrast, the driest parts

of the country—for example, the coastal plains of the Lesser Sunda islands and parts of Java— have annual rainfall of less than 39 inches (1,000 mm). Some years the rainfall can be exceedingly low and crops can fail.

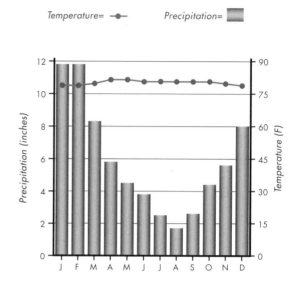

Temperature= ─●─   Precipitation= ▮

▲ Average monthly climate conditions in Jakarta

▼ This young girl uses a large banana leaf to protect herself from the heavy tropical rain in Lombok. Brief but heavy rainstorms occur most days in Indonesia's coastal regions.

CHAPTER 4

Population and Settlements

Indonesia has the world's fourth-largest population. In 2006, its population stood at over 245 million, and it is increasing at a rate of 1.5 percent per year. About 29 percent of the country's population is under 14 years old, which means that Indonesia's population will continue to increase for some time to come. In contrast, Britain's population increased just 0.24 percent in 2005, and less than 18 percent of its population is under 14.

Although Indonesia's population is growing quickly, its rate of increase has slowed down slightly from a high of 1.8 percent per year during the 1980s. A number of factors have caused this small reduction in growth, including improvements in education and the government's successful family planning program.

MIGRATION TO THE CITIES

Indonesia's population is unevenly distributed. Some areas are heavily populated while others have a small population. For example, 60 percent of Indonesia's population (about 145 million people) live on Java, Bali and Madura, but these islands represent just 7 percent of the land area. Papua has 22 percent of the land area but barely 1 percent of the population.

Since the 1970s, many people in Indonesia have migrated from rural areas to the cities in search of work. The country, therefore, has a large urban population. By 2003, 46 percent of Indonesia's population lived in urban areas, compared to 22 percent in 1980. During the late 1990s, the country's urban population grew at about 3.6 percent per year, more than twice as fast as the population in rural areas. This rapid

▶ Most houses in Indonesia are built on stilts. These houses are on Sumbawa Island. Stilts prevent the houses from flooding during heavy rains and provide ventilation. The space under the house is also used for storage.

growth means that most cities are overcrowded and their infrastructure is unable to cope. The migrants often end up living in large squatter settlements that have sprung up around the cities, where there are makeshift houses but no services such as water and electricity.

MAJOR SETTLEMENTS

Jakarta, located in western Java, is Indonesia's capital city, with a population of more than 13 million. It is the country's main center for industry and commerce. Other major cities in Indonesia include Surabaya, in east Java, which

► Jakarta has many slum areas where people live crowded together in very poor conditions. These shacks stand on stilts beside a dirty canal. Although this water is polluted with sewage, it is probably used for washing, cleaning, and cooking.

Population Data

📂 Population: over 245 million

📂 Population 0–14 yrs: 29%

📂 Population 15–64 yrs: 66%

📂 Population 65+ yrs: 5%

📂 Population growth rate: 1.5%

📂 Population density: 300.6 per sq mile/ 116.1 per sq km

📂 Urban population: 46%

📂 Major cities: Jakarta 13,194,000
                  Bandung 4,020,000
                  Surabaya 2,735,000

Source: United Nations and World Bank

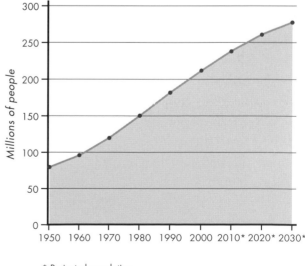

* Projected population

▲ Population growth, 1950–2030

▲ The Dayak people live in Borneo. Each village builds a few large community long-houses using wood, bamboo, and palm leaves. This Dayak woman is weaving a basket from palm leaves.

has about 4 million people and is an industrial center and port. Semarang, in central Java, is a major port and commercial center for the region. Bandung, in west Java, is an important center for technology and aircraft building. Medan, in northern Sumatra, is a growing industrial center based on agriculture and low-cost energy. Makassar is the capital city of south Sulawesi and the main gateway to eastern Indonesia.

ETHNIC GROUPS

People of many ethnic groups live in Indonesia. The largest of these groups is the Javanese, who make up 45 percent of the population and live mainly in central and eastern Java. The Sundanese live at the western end of Java and make up 14 percent of the country's population. Other important groups include the Madurese, from Madura, who make up 7.5 percent of the population; and the ethnic Malay, who are spread through several areas and make up another 7.5 percent of Indonesia's population.

Among the ethnic groups on Sumatra are the Acehnese, from the north; Bataks, from around Lake Toba; and the Minangkabau, from the western highlands. A number of ethnic groups live on Sulawesi, including the Minahasans, the Makassarese, and the Bugis, who are known as seafarers and who live along the southern coasts. Kalimantan is populated by more than 200 groups, most of which are either tribes of the Dayak people or ethnic Malays. Several million Indonesian Chinese also live in the country. These people emigrated to Indonesia from China. Some of them have been settled in Indonesia for many generations, while others have arrived recently.

ETHNIC TENSIONS

Tension has long existed between Indonesian Chinese and other Indonesians. Indonesian Chinese live mostly in the country's urban areas. Traditionally, they have been successful in business and enjoy a higher standard of living than other Indonesians. This has led to resentment by other Indonesians. During 1997 and 1998, many Indonesians blamed the Chinese for the country's economic problems, and violent clashes occurred that caused many thousands of Chinese to flee the country.

Violence has also flared up between Christians and Muslims in western Java, Ambon, and parts of the Moluccas. Three years of fighting in the Moluccas killed about 5,000 people and caused 750,000 people to flee the islands. The fighting finally ended in 2002, when the two sides signed a peace deal. Ethnic violence has also occurred in Kalimantan, where the native Dayak people have resented the influx of migrants from Madura as part of the government's transmigration program.

Focus on: Transmigration

Beginning in the 1950s, Indonesia's transmigration program has moved families from the overcrowded regions of Java to less densely populated islands. In the early 1970s, the program gained the support of international donors, such as the World Bank. Since then, hundreds of thousands of families have been moved to Sumatra, Kalimantan, Sulawesi, Maluku, and Papua. Many of the region's indigenous people have resented the migrants, and there have been violent clashes. In 2001, the Dayaks of Kalimantan killed thousands of Madurese migrants, and the government was forced to evacuate many Madurese for their own safety. The government also let the migrants down by making promises of land, services, schools, and transportation, many of which were not fulfilled. In 2000, the program was halted because of rising costs and a shortage of suitable sites for resettlement, but tensions between indigenous peoples and the migrants continue.

▼ Most food in Indonesia is bought and sold at traditional open air markets.

CHAPTER 5

Government and Politics

The government of Indonesia is faced with the challenge of balancing the needs of a very diverse country and maintaining unity. It also needs to tackle the problems of widespread corruption, human rights abuses, and demands from several provinces for more self-rule or independence. Other issues facing the government include poverty and terrorism.

GOVERNMENT ORGANIZATION

Indonesia's government operates under a constitution that was first established in 1945. It is based on Pancasila, or the Five Principles. These principles include a belief in one god, a just and civilized society, the unity of Indonesia, democracy, and social justice for all Indonesians.

Changes have been made to the constitution over the years. The most significant change came in 2002. This change allowed the people to directly elect the president and altered the structure of the People's Consultative Assembly to allow more regional representation.

Indonesia's president is the country's chief of state, its head of government, and the supreme commander-in-chief of its armed forces. The country's national legislature is the People's

▼ President Susilo Bambang Yudhoyono (left) came to power in 2004. In May 2005, he met President George W. Bush for talks at the White House, in Washington, D.C.

Consultative Assembly. It is made up of two chambers: the House of Representatives (Dewan Perwakilan Rakyat, or DPR) and the Regional Representatives' Council (Dewan Perwakilan Daerah, or DPD). The DPR is the more powerful chamber; it approves the country's laws and submits bills to the president for approval. The DPD was created in 2004 to represent the provinces; its authority is limited to regional issues. Each of the provinces has a governor appointed by the president and an equal number of democratically elected representatives. The provinces are subdivided into districts (*kabupaten*) and subdistricts (*kecamatan*). In order to decentralize the government, the districts have been given more responsibilities including health, education, agriculture, transportation, industry, and the environment.

POLITICAL ORGANIZATIONS

While President Suharto was in power, the country had three political organizations:

▲ A woman votes in the presidential election in October 2004. This was the first election in which Indonesians directly elected a president.

Golkar (the ruling political organization), the Muslim-backed Development Unity Party (Partai Persatuan Pembangunan, or PPP), and the Indonesian Democratic Party (Partai Demokrasi Indonesia, or PDI). Since Suharto's fall in 1998, more than 100 new political parties have been formed, including the Democratic Party led by Susilo Bambang Yudhoyono.

CORRUPTION

Corruption has been a problem in Indonesia since independence. About U.S.$2.35 billion are believed to have been "lost" as a result of the misuse of state funds and bribery. Some groups claim that President Suharto was the most corrupt political leader anywhere in the world for the past 20 years. The government elected in Indonesia in 2004 has taken action to stamp out corruption.

REGIONAL SELF-RULE

One of the constitution's Five Principles, national unity, is being challenged by several provinces that want more self-rule. One of these provinces is Papua. The Free Papua Movement, a separatist group, has been fighting for independence since the 1960s. In 2002, the government of Megawati Sukarnoputri approved self-rule for Papua, giving the province control over its day-to-day affairs. The government also allowed Papua to keep much of the revenue from its natural resources and to change its name from Irian Jaya to Papua. However, the government has failed to establish self-rule for Papua. Instead, the province has been divided into two and allowed to have a directly elected governor and a regional legislature. In 2005, Indonesia's government set up the Papuan People's Council to represent the views of the tribal peoples but little progress has been made toward self-rule, and the unrest continues. The influx of large numbers of migrants and of people fleeing conflict in other parts of Indonesia has added to the problems in Papua. The indigenous Papuans are mostly rural and Christian, while most of the migrants are urban and Muslim. There are many conflicting interests among these groups.

In the strongly conservative Muslim province of Aceh, an increase in self-rule has resulted in the adoption of Sharia, or Islamic law. Indonesia's government is not an Islamic government that follows Sharia law, but many of its members are Muslims. In 2002, the government of Indonesia allowed the provincial government of Aceh formally to adopt Sharia, which had been used unofficially for many years. This strict Muslim code of law has specific rules on alcohol, clothing, and personal conduct.

▼ Although these Papuan tribal people live in the remote village of Jiwika, located in the highlands of Papua, they were still able to vote in the parliamentary elections of April 2004. Some Papuans traveled for many days to reach a polling place.

HUMAN RIGHTS

The government elected to power in Indonesia in 2004 campaigned on human rights issues. Groups such as Human Rights Watch (an international nongovernmental organization) have found evidence that the country still has a number of obstacles to overcome. For example, members of Indonesia's armed forces continue to carry out arrests and beatings of civilians, detainees are tortured while they are in police and military custody, and protesters in Aceh and Papua are badly treated. The country's legal system is still corrupt. This type of corruption means members of the police and the military are often not held to account for their actions.

▶ These women, who were photographed in 2001, are members of the Free Aceh Movement. They have been trained to use weapons, and they fight alongside the male separatists. Over the years, support for their separatist movement has grown. Indonesia's government has moved additional troops into the region to fight against the rebels.

Focus on: Tribal rights

The traditional way of life of many indigenous people in Indonesia is under threat from the influx of migrants and extensive deforestation. Often the rights of indigenous people are ignored. In order to have a bigger voice in politics, the different indigenous peoples of Indonesia have formed an alliance. In 1999, they set up the Aliansi Masyarakat Adat Nusantara (AMAN), or the Indigenous People's Alliance of the Archipelago. This alliance is supported by a number of international nongovernmental organizations. Many of Indonesia's indigenous groups were affected by the tsunami of December 2004. AMAN has worked to make sure that the survivors are not resettled away from their tribal lands and that their way of life is preserved. AMAN is also campaigning for more self-rule for indigenous people, and it is working to ensure that they have more control over the management of their natural resources.

CHAPTER 6

Energy and Resources

Indonesia is rich in natural resources. The country has oil and natural gas fields, as well as reserves of tin, bauxite, copper, and precious metals. It also has extensive forests and rich soils for agriculture.

OIL AND GAS

Most of Indonesia's oil and natural gas is found along the coast of Sumatra, in Kalimantan, and in the seas around it. In 2005, Indonesia produced about 80 percent of Southeast Asia's oil. About 33 percent of the world's liquefied gas comes from Indonesia's gas fields. The country's government controls all oil and gas exploration and production through Pertamina, the state-owned oil company. The foreign companies that operate in Indonesia, which are mostly from Europe and North America, must have partnership agreements with Pertamina.

Indonesia's oil production reached a peak of about 1.5 million barrels a day during the late 1990s. Since then, production has fallen to 1.07 million barrels per day. This is because some of the older oil fields have dried up, and there has been a lack of foreign investment. Because domestic demand for oil has risen, Indonesia is now a net importer of oil. This costs the economy U.S.$1.2 billion each year. Unless

? Did You Know?

The oil industry in Indonesia is one of the oldest in the world. Oil was discovered in northern Sumatra in 1883. Its discovery led to the formation of a new oil company called the Royal Dutch Company for Exploration of Petroleum Sources in the Netherlands Indies. In 1907, this company merged with Shell Transport and Trading Company, a British company that was searching for oil in Kalimantan. The new company was called Royal Dutch Shell. Today, Royal Dutch Shell is one of the world's leading oil companies.

◀ During the 1970s, a large natural gas field was discovered off the coast of Aceh, near the town of Lhokseumawe. After this discovery, a huge oil terminal and petrochemical complex was built there.

new oil fields are discovered, it is likely that Indonesia's oil reserves will run out by 2020. Gas production, however, is high. In 2002, Indonesia produced 2.5 trillion cubic feet (70.4 billion cubic meters) of natural gas.

MINING

Mining contributes about 10 percent to Indonesia's Gross Domestic Product (GDP). After Malaysia, Indonesia is the world's largest producer of tin. Most of its tin reserves are found on the islands of Bangka and Belitung. Bauxite (the ore for aluminum) is produced on Bintan Island; coal is mined on Sumatra; nickel on Sulawesi; and copper, silver, and gold on Papua. Indonesia has increased its production of minerals by establishing joint ventures with companies from the United States and Britain. British Petroleum (BP) and Rio Tinto, for example, carry out most of the coal mining.

▶ Workers extract sulphur from the slopes of an active volcano in east Java. They dig the lumps of yellow sulphur out by hand and carry them down the slopes in baskets to a collection point. Although this job is hazardous, the workers wear no protection. Factories buy the sulphur stones for use in manufacturing.

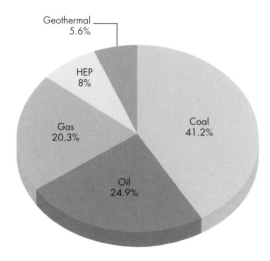

▲ Electricity production by type

Geothermal 5.6%
HEP 8%
Gas 20.3%
Coal 41.2%
Oil 24.9%

Energy Data

▱ Energy consumption as % of world total: 1.4%

▱ Energy consumption by sector (% of total):
  Industry: 18.5
  Transportation: 18.7
  Agriculture: 1.7
  Services: 1.4
  Residential: 58.8
  Other: 0.9

▱ CO_2 emissions as % of world total: 1.2

▱ CO_2 emissions per capita in tons per year: 1.5

Source: World Resources Institute

ALTERNATIVE ENERGY SOURCES

Indonesia's government is eager to develop alternative energy sources to reduce dependence on fossil fuels and help tackle the problem of air pollution. Hydroelectric power (HEP) provides about 8 percent of the country's electricity. One of Indonesia's largest HEP dams is on the Asahan River in Sumatra. Given the country's mountainous landscape and high rainfall, it has great potential for generating HEP. Small-scale HEP projects are important because they can provide power to remote mountain villages that lack electricity. As a result of government grants, small wind turbines and photovoltaic panels (panels that convert light energy into electricity) have been supplied to some villages. Biogas is another important source of energy, especially in Indonesia's rural areas. It is a mix of gases produced by rotting organic wastes in an underground chamber. Biogas can be used for cooking and heating.

AGRICULTURE

About one-fifth of Indonesia's land is either cultivated for crops or used for timber plantations. In 2005, agriculture accounted for 15 percent of the country's GDP. The country's many small farms provide much of its food. Rice is Indonesia's staple food, and in 2004, the country grew about 58 million tons (53 million metric tons) of it. Other important crops in Indonesia are cassava, coconuts, maize, peanuts, sweet potatoes, soybeans, and sugarcane. A number of high-value crops are grown for export on large agricultural estates. Indonesia is the world's largest producer of cloves, the second-largest producer of rubber, and the fourth-largest coffee grower. Other export crops include tea, cocoa, tobacco, sugar, and palm oil.

▼ Farmers work the slopes near the village of Ubud by hand. They work by hand because it is difficult to get machinery onto the terraces.

FISHING

Indonesia has a large fishing industry. Its total catch in 2001 was 5.6 million tons (5.1 million metric tons), of which one-quarter came from fresh water. The catch includes tuna, carp, anchovies, and scad, as well as shrimp and prawns. About 90 percent of the country's fishers use traditional methods, such as nets, hooks, and lines; their fish is caught and sold locally. The remaining 10 percent are commercial fishers with large boats. This group accounts for half the catch, most of which is exported. The production of farmed prawns for the European market has increased, and coastal mangrove swamps have been cleared to make space for the prawn ponds.

FORESTRY

Just under 60 percent of Indonesia is covered in hardwood forest, much of which is state owned. Indonesia is a major exporter of tropical hardwood, and it is the largest exporter of plywood. Most of the forests are not managed in a sustainable way, and the careful maintenance of this valuable resource is one of Indonesia's most pressing issues. Demand for wood has increased, especially from other Asian countries such as China and Japan. This demand, along with deregulation of the trade in unfinished wood products such as plywood, has resulted in even more felling of trees in the country. Illegal logging is a major problem. The prevention of illegal logging is difficult. The developed countries that buy illegal wood products could do much to stop these exports by boycotting timber that does not come from legally logged forests. Also, consumers could check the source of any timber they buy. The Indonesian Ecolabeling Institute is setting up a timber certification program that will indicate timber that comes from sustainably managed forests.

▲ This woman is planting teak tree seedlings at Walanbenote Community Teak Tree Nursery on Muna Island, in Sulawesi. It is important that felled trees are replaced to ensure the supply of timber for the future.

Focus on: Bird Flu

Indonesia has millions of chickens and ducks, many of which are kept in the backyards of homes. The H5N1 strain of avian influenza—better known as "bird flu"—arrived in Indonesia in late 2003 and has since spread across two-thirds of the country. It has killed millions of birds, including those kept for the poultry trade. Indonesia is preparing an early bird flu warning system to speed up the reporting of any outbreaks.

CHAPTER 7

Economy and Income

During the 1980s and 1990s, Indonesia's economy grew, mostly as a result of its supply of cheap oil and gas. By the mid-1990s, Indonesia had one of the best-performing Asian economies. It suffered a major setback, however, in 1997 because of the Asian Currency Crisis. Indonesia's economy started to recover in 2000, and by 2005, its annual growth rate had risen to 5 percent, similar to that of Malaysia.

much more expensive. At first, the government subsidized the price of fuel to keep costs down. But as global oil prices increased in 2005, the predicted cost of the subsidies rose to a staggering U.S.$11 billion. In October 2005, the government responded to this situation by raising the cost of fuel in the country by 126 percent. This increase caused Indonesia's inflation rate to rise to 17 percent in 2006—and its economic growth to fall.

MANUFACTURING AND INDUSTRY

Indonesia's industrial and manufacturing sector has grown over the last 40 years. In 2005, it contributed 44 percent to the country's GDP. Indonesia's main industries are oil, natural gas, mining, cement, chemical fertilizers, rubber, and timber. Oil and gas were once major sources of export earnings, but in 2004, Indonesia became a net importer of oil. The country had been used to cheap supplies of fuel, but the imported oil was

SERVICE INDUSTRIES

Another major area of Indonesia's economy is its service sector, which contributes 41 percent to the country's GDP. This sector is expanding fast and is made up of government services, transportation, communications, finance, tourism, and food. There are a large number of workers in this industry, but many, such as the drivers of motorized taxis, street vendors, and garbage recyclers, are poorly paid. Most of these workers have little job security.

◀ Indonesia's manufacturing sector is an important earner of foreign income. These athletic shoes are being made at a factory at Tangerang, on Java, in 2006. They will be exported to Europe and North America.

▶ In 2005, the clean-up following the tsunami was a massive operation. These boys are collecting oil drums that have washed up on the coast near an oil refinery. The oil company pays them for every drum they find.

Economic Data

🗁 Gross National Income (GNI) in U.S.$: 248,007,000,000

🗁 World rank by GNI: 22

🗁 GNI per capita in U.S.$: 1,140

🗁 World rank by GNI per capita: 137

🗁 Economic growth: 5%

Source: World Bank

GROWING WORKFORCE

Indonesia's main areas of employment are agriculture (40 percent), services (38 percent), and industry (17 percent). Women make up about 40 percent of the country's workforce. The rapidly expanding population means that the workforce is also growing. In 2003, Indonesia's total workforce was 107 million, up from 60 million in 1980. Each year, several million new jobs are needed if the country's unemployment rate is not to increase.

Focus on: The Asian Currency Crisis

In 1997, international concern grew over the fact that many of the fast-growing Asian countries—including Indonesia—had very large debts. This concern caused a fall in the value of the rupiah, the Indonesian currency. The fall in the value of the rupiah, in turn, made it more difficult for the government and businesses to pay their foreign loans. Many businesses went bankrupt, and millions of people lost their jobs. The International Monetary Fund (IMF) rescued Indonesia with a massive loan, but, in exchange for the loan, the government had to work to cut spending and reform the country's financial sector. Indonesia's crisis deepened in 1998 when the IMF claimed that Suharto was not carrying out the reforms, and the loan was stopped. Inflation in Indonesia soared, more than one-half of the country's population was living in poverty, and there were demonstrations in the cities. Eventually, in May 1998, Suharto resigned. Since then, Indonesia's economy has slowly recovered, but the country's level of poverty remains high.

Most of Indonesia's manufacturing industries are based in Java, where the dense population provides the workforce and where there is a reasonable transportation network. The country's government is attempting to direct investment and job creation away from Java by establishing free-trade and industrial zones elsewhere. The main zone of this type is Batam Island, which lies across the Straits of Malacca from Singapore, a small country located on the tip of mainland Malaysia. Batam Island quickly developed into an international port and industrial center, and it is one of the country's wealthiest cities. It has already attracted substantial foreign investment, and it is expanding rapidly; in 2003, it grew by more than 30 percent. Similar zones are being considered for Kalimantan and Sulawesi.

MIGRANT WORKERS

The increase in the size of the country's workforce and its lack of jobs has forced millions of Indonesians to look for work overseas. This is especially true in the case of women, who make up 75 percent of all Indonesian migrant workers. The money that migrant workers send back to their families represents important revenue for the economy. As many as 1.5 million Indonesians work in Malaysia, but there are thousands of others working in the Middle East, Hong Kong, and Singapore. Men work in construction and agriculture, while women usually work as cleaners and cooks in private houses. These jobs are usually low paid and the hours are long. For example, about 200,000 Indonesian domestic workers work in Malaysia. They typically work up to 18 hours a day, seven days a week, and earn less than U.S.$0.25 per hour. Many are forbidden to leave their workplace and some employers refuse to pay their workers until the end of their contract. Employment agencies in Indonesia arrange the jobs, but they are poorly regulated and ignore the abuse of the workers.

▼ A number of major car manufacturers have assembly plants in Indonesia. This worker is welding parts to a car frame at the Japanese-owned Honda factory in Karawang in west Java. Car sales in Indonesia have fallen, and the workforce in this industry is being reduced.

In addition, many Indonesians illegally migrate to other countries to find work without the proper documents. These illegal workers suffer even more abuse than other migrant workers.

RISING POVERTY

About 10 percent of Indonesia's workforce are unemployed, and an estimated 16.7 percent live below the poverty line of less than U.S.$17 a month. The country's government is trying to tackle poverty using poverty reduction committees that work within communities. These committees give government grants to the poorest villages to help them to develop and to help individuals learn new skills and set up businesses. Finance programs have been set up to offer farmers loans so they can develop their land.

? Did You Know?

Indonesia's government intends to spend about U.S.$1.5 billion in 2007 on improving conditions in about 70,000 villages and subdistricts. This will create about five million new jobs.

▲ Many illegal Indonesian migrants work in Malaysia. In October 2004, Malaysia's government ran an amnesty program that encouraged illegal migrants to return to Indonesia. After returning to Indonesia, they would then be able to obtain the necessary documents to become legal workers.

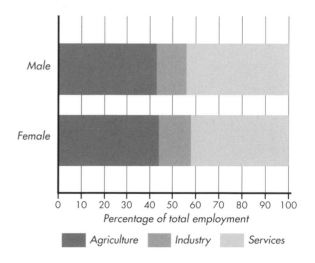

Percentage of total employment

Agriculture   Industry   Services

▲ Labor force by sector and gender

CHAPTER 8

Global Connections

Until 2004, Indonesia's relationships with some of its close neighbors, especially Australia and Malaysia, were chilly. The authoritarian government of Suharto was suspicious of other countries and did not encourage close ties. Since the 2004 elections, Indonesia has been trying to improve its international standing. The country's president has participated in international summits such as the Association of Southeast Asian Nations (ASEAN) and Asia Pacific Economic Cooperation (APEC) summits and has held talks with neighboring countries.

TERRITORIAL DISPUTES

Indonesia has far more coastline than most other countries (about 34,000 miles/54,716 km). In 1980, it claimed for itself all the waters surrounding its islands to a distance of about 13.7 miles (22 km) from the coastline. In addition, it claimed an exclusive economic zone extending 230 miles (370 km) in which it controlled fishing and geological rights. Not surprisingly, this move caused territorial disputes with its neighbors. Australia disputed Indonesia's rights to the continental shelf off the coast of Timor, an issue that was finally resolved in 1991 with an agreement that allowed Australia and Indonesia joint access to the area. Disputes over boundaries between Indonesia and Singapore were settled in 2005.

In 2002, Indonesia and Malaysia took their territorial dispute over the Sipadan and Ligitan Islands, which are located off the coast of Kalimantan, to the International Court of Justice. The court decided in favor of Malaysia, but since then there have been further disputes

► In November 2005, the leaders of the Asia Pacific Economic Cooperation summit met in Pusan, South Korea, to discuss a range of issues, including their response to a possible epidemic of bird flu. In the foreground are Prime Minister Junichiro Koizumi of Japan (wearing gray robe) and President Susilo Bambang Yudhoyono of Indonesia (wearing yellow robe, standing on the right).

over the rich oil deposits in the seas around the islands. Warships from both countries moved into the area in 2005. Malaysia is managing the islands, but this is still disputed by Indonesia.

Indonesia's dispute with China over the Natuna Islands in the South China Sea is still not resolved. In 1993, China presented a map of its claims to territories in the South China Sea. The map included the Natuna Islands together with much of the economic zone claimed by Indonesia. Because the gas reserves in this region are among the largest in the world, both countries are claiming the territory.

PIRACY AND TERRORISM

The Straits of Malacca between northern Sumatra, Malaysia, and Singapore are one of the busiest shipping lanes in the world. They have been a subject of dispute for years. Indonesia and Malaysia lay joint claim to the waters while other countries, notably the United States, consider them to be international

▲ In the Straits of Malacca, naval patrols have been increased to stop the threat of piracy. These Indonesians were "arrested" as part of a naval exercise involving Indonesia, Malaysia, and Singapore in May 2000.

waters. Most countries would prefer the straits to be classed as international waters because of their importance to world trade. The threat of piracy is forcing Indonesia, Malaysia, and Singapore to put aside their differences and work together. Piracy has been a problem in the straits for hundreds of years, but recently the number of attacks has increased. In 2000, a record 220 attacks took place. There are also fears that terrorists could target the straits; it would be relatively easy to sink a ship in the shallowest part and block the shipping lane. As a result, Indonesia, Malaysia, and Singapore have agreed to join forces and patrol the straits.

Indonesia has suffered from several terrorist attacks since 2002, including bombings in Bali

◀ On October 12, 2002, bombs exploded in a nightclub area in the popular tourist resort of Kuta on the island of Bali. Over 200 people were killed and many more were injured. In this picture, emergency workers remove victims from the scene.

in 2002 and 2005, the bombing of the Marriott Hotel in Jakarta in 2003, and the bombing of the Australian Embassy in 2004.

Countries such as United States and Australia have urged Indonesia to address the threat of terrorism. The United States in particular has encouraged Indonesia to take an active role in regional security and has provided it with military assistance. This assistance is given on the condition that Indonesia improves its human-rights record. Since 2002, Indonesia's police force has arrested and successfully charged 40 terrorists, most of whom were Indonesian Islamic radicals linked to Al-Qaeda.

WORKING WITH AUSTRALIA

Indonesia's relationship with Australia, one of its close neighbors, has had its ups and downs. The government of Suharto was deeply suspicious of Australia because Australia supported the people of Aceh and East Timor.

In 1999, Australia led the UN peacekeeping force in East Timor. The 2002 Bali bombing killed 88 Australians, more than any other single event in the country since World War II, and this led to close cooperation between the police forces of Australia and Indonesia. Further improvements occurred in 2005, when President Yudhoyono and Australian Prime Minister John Howard agreed to cooperate in fighting terrorism, drugs, illegal migration, and the smuggling of people. In 2006, however, relations between the two countries reached a low when Australia granted

? Did You Know?

Since the 2004 tsunami, international efforts have been made to set up an early warning system to give countries time to evacuate their citizens from at-risk areas. Two early warning buoys have been deployed off the coast of Sumatra. These buoys are connected to pressure sensors on the seabed that detect any movement caused by earthquakes.

asylum to a group of 42 refugees from Papua who claimed that the military was carrying out genocide against the Papuan people. Indonesia's government claimed that this move was giving support to the separatist movement in Papua and demanded the refugees be returned. Australia responded by granting the Papuans a protection visa that allows that the Papuans to stay in Australia for three years.

ASEAN

A major part of Indonesia's foreign policy is its membership in the Association of Southeast Asian Nations (ASEAN), an organization formed in 1967 by Indonesia, Thailand, Malaysia, Singapore, and the Philippines to work on economic, social, and cultural issues. Since then, Brunei, Vietnam, Laos, Myanmar, and Cambodia have also become members.

▶ On November 14, 2003, Australian United Nations peacekeepers lowered the UN flag during a farewell ceremony in Suai district, in East Timor, at the end of their tour of duty.

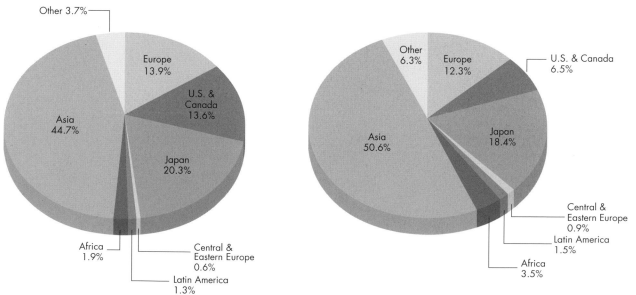

Other 3.7%
Europe 13.9%
U.S. & Canada 13.6%
Asia 44.7%
Japan 20.3%
Africa 1.9%
Central & Eastern Europe 0.6%
Latin America 1.3%

▲ Destination of exports by major trading region

Other 6.3%
Europe 12.3%
U.S. & Canada 6.5%
Asia 50.6%
Japan 18.4%
Central & Eastern Europe 0.9%
Latin America 1.5%
Africa 3.5%

▲ Origin of imports by major trading region

CHAPTER 9

Transportation and Communications

Traveling around Indonesia can be difficult because of the number of islands and their mountainous interiors. Nevertheless, good inter-island transportation is essential to the economy of the country.

ISLAND-TO-ISLAND TRAVEL

Air services in Indonesia fly between about 470 local airports, although some of these are little more than dirt landing strips. The national carrier is Garuda, which has international and domestic routes. Merpati Nusantara Airlines has mostly domestic routes and some international routes.

Ferries and other sea links are a common means of traveling between the islands. More than 300 ports are registered for international and interisland trade, including Palembang, Batam, Cirebon, Jakarta, Kupang, Semarang, Surabaya, and Makassar. Frequent ferries run between neighboring islands and across the Straits of Malacca to Malaysia and Singapore. In addition, more than 4,000 traditional sailing boats and about 1,000 motorized vessels carry goods and passengers among the islands.

Indonesia has about 13,670 miles (22,000 km) of inland rivers and other waterways. Boat services on these waterways provide essential transportation to the inland regions. The only way to reach the remote interior of Kalimantan, for example, is to use a long-boat, or a shallow boat fitted with a high-powered engine.

◄ The 2004 tsunami destroyed the coastal road that connected Banda Aceh and other towns with the rest of Sumatra. In 2005, a new ferry service was set up from Banda Aceh for transportation.

▶ Although travel on the commuter trains into Jakarta is relatively cheap, many people prefer to travel for free by sitting on the roof or clinging to the sides. Unfortunately, a number of people fall to their deaths each year.

RAILWAYS AND ROAD

Indonesian State Railways operates a limited train network serving Java and parts of Sumatra. The main route is between Jakarta and Surabaya but there are also rail links between Jakarta and Semarang, Yogyakarta, and Solo. Commuter trains called *kereta api* run several times daily between Bogor and Jakarta. These trains are crowded and dirty, and many people sit on top of them to avoid paying fares.

Outside the main cities, Indonesia's road network is poor. Many of the roads in the country's rural areas are little more than dirt tracks. Long-distance bus services link most of the major cities. It is possible to travel all the way from Banda Aceh in western Sumatra to Bali, although the trip takes several days and involves numerous buses and ferries.

CITY TRANSPORTATION

Most of Indonesia's cities suffer from traffic congestion. City transportation is varied and includes cars, taxis, buses, mopeds, and numerous *bajaj* and *becaks*. *Bajaj* are motorized rickshaws that carry between two and five passengers.

Transport & Communications Data

- 🗀 Total roads: 228,899 miles/368,360 km
- 🗀 Total paved roads: 132,761 miles/ 213,649 km
- 🗀 Total unpaved roads: 96,137 miles/ 154,711 km
- 🗀 Total railways: 4,013 miles/6,458 km
- 🗀 Major airports, paved runways: 161
- 🗀 Cars per 1,000 people: 12
- 🗀 Cellular phones per 1,000 people: 138
- 🗀 Personal computers per 1,000 people: 14
- 🗀 Internet users per 1,000 people: 67

Source: World Bank and CIA World Factbook

There are more than 20,000 *bajaj* in Jakarta alone, and each one is restricted to traveling in a specific part of the city. *Becaks* are human-powered rickshaws that were banned from Jakarta in 1994, because they often caused traffic problems. They are still found in other cities. Indonesia also has minibuses that carry ten or more passengers; these buses are a common way of traveling between the city center and the suburbs.

COMMUNICATIONS

In the past it was almost impossible to establish a good communications network across Indonesia, and many remote villages were cut off from the rest of the country. New technologies such as satellite phones, cellular phones, and the Internet are changing communications in Indonesia. Today, it is possible for villagers in remote places such as Kalimantan to have satellite phones and Internet access. Cellular phone coverage in the country is also improving, especially in the rural areas. These developments also enable people to keep in contact with family members who are working overseas.

MEDIA AND THE INTERNET

Until 1990, Indonesia's television and radio networks were controlled by the government through the state-owned TV station, TVRI. Now, there are more than 40 private TV stations, and they provide viewers with a greater choice of programs. In the past, Suharto's government maintained a tight control on newspapers and magazines and censored any content that was critical of either

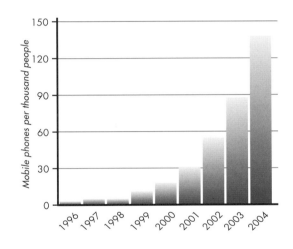

▲ Cellular phone use, 1996–2004

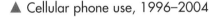

◀ As in Europe and North America, the cellular phone has become a popular item among young people.

► About two-thirds of Indonesian people use Internet cafés, such as this one in Jakarta.

the president or the government. In 1994, the government withdrew the licenses of three of the country's leading magazines because of articles they had published. Since Suharto left office in 1998, censorship has been relaxed, and the country has many more publications.

Focus on: Jakarta's Traffic Problems

Jakarta has a massive traffic congestion problem, which is caused by the four million or so vehicles that crowd its streets. These vehicles are also responsible for much of the air pollution in the city. Since 1992, a "three-in-one" rule has been in operation during rush hour. According to this rule, access to certain roads is restricted to cars with three or more passengers. The city has also started an ambitious program to build a rapid transit system made up of a subway network, new railway links, a monorail, and bus routes. Construction on the bus routes started in 2003. These massive engineering projects caused even more traffic congestion. Eventually, the new measures began to work. Today, the bus routes are attracting thousands more passengers each year.

Indonesia's first Internet service became available in 1995. Since then, access to the Internet in the country has increased, and it has numerous online services including those that offer newspapers and shopping in the national language, Bahasa Indonesia. The amount of Internet access in Indonesia, however, is far behind that of Singapore and Malaysia. This is because few Indonesians own their own computers. Between 60 and 70 percent of Internet access in Indonesia is provided by Internet cafés. Debate exists in Indonesia at both national and local levels about whether it is necessary to restrict access to certain kinds of Web sites, such as those showing pornography and those linked to terrorist groups.

? Did You Know?

In 2005, President Yudhoyono told a small meeting of people that if they thought the government did not care about their problems they should call him on his cellular phone. He gave out his number, which was broadcast everywhere by the media. Within minutes, the president's mobile phone was overwhelmed with a variety of complaints!

CHAPTER 10

Education and Health

The size of Indonesia's population puts pressure on the country's social services, such as education and health care. Indonesia is faced with the challenge of providing education and health care to a young and growing population, many of whom live in poverty.

PRIMARY SCHOOLING

An important government goal following independence was to provide every child with at least six years of primary schooling. This goal has been achieved. During the 1970s, some of Indonesia's oil revenue was used to build new primary schools and fund education programs. By the late 1980s, about 40,000 primary schools had either been built or had their existing buildings improved. This gave a new generation of schoolchildren a firm foundation for their education. During the 1990s, these children progressed through the educational system. As a

result of these educational programs, Indonesia's literacy is relatively high; 94 percent of adult males and 86 percent of adult females are now literate. Quality of education, however, varies within the country, and supplying adequate facilities, well-qualified teachers, and textbooks in remote areas remains a problem.

Since 1990, compulsory education in Indonesia has included six years of primary schooling. About 87 percent of the country's children begin primary school at six years old. Primary school in Indonesia is not completely free; parents have to pay for books and uniforms. Most schools have classes in the morning, and all children are expected to do several hours of homework. Primary school children attend a special class in school to study Pancasila, the guiding principles of Indonesian society. They must pass exams in this class in order to

◀ In 2005, children play outside their Islamic primary school on the outskirts of Banda Aceh.

► A teacher helps students with their classwork at a secondary school in Timor.

progress to the next grade. Islamic schools, called madrasas, are growing in popularity in the country because they offer free education. However, students in madrasas are taught only about Islam and the Koran.

SECONDARY SCHOOL AND BEYOND

Slightly fewer than 60 percent of Indonesia's primary school children continue to junior secondary school for three years. By 2008, the three years of junior secondary school will also be compulsory for all students. Students who complete junior secondary school can then go to secondary school for an additional three years, assuming they pass the entrance exam. After completing secondary school, they can go to a university. University courses in Indonesia, however, are very expensive; generally, only the wealthier students can afford them. Indonesia has more than 50 state-run universities and more than 1,000 private universities. Its largest and most important universities are the University of Indonesia, in Jakarta; Gajah

Mada University, in Yogyakarta; and Padjadjaran University, in Bandung. In the past, more boys attended school in Indonesia than girls, but in 2005, the percentage of boys and girls attending primary and junior secondary school was very similar. Slightly fewer girls than boys go on to higher education in the country.

Education and Health Data

- ◠ Life expectancy at birth, male: 65.5
- ◠ Life expectancy at birth, female: 69.3
- ◠ Infant mortality rate per 1,000: 31
- ◠ Under five mortality rate per 1,000: 41
- ◠ Physicians per 1,000 people: 0.1
- ◠ Health expenditure as % of GDP: 3%
- ◠ Education expenditure as % of GDP: 1%
- ◠ Primary-school net enrollment: 87%
- ◠ Student-teacher ratio, primary: 20
- ◠ Adult literacy as % age 15+: 90

Source: United Nations Agencies and World Bank

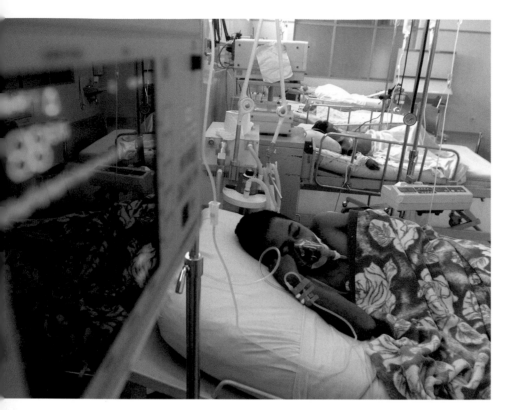

◀ These patients in a hospital in Jakarta are being treated for dengue fever. In 2004 there was an outbreak of dengue fever, a disease carried by the mosquito. Several hundred people died and many thousands were infected before the outbreak was brought under control.

HEALTH

In recent years, Indonesia's government has focused on providing basic health care to the country's population to reduce the high death rate among young children. Improvements have been achieved using public health centers called *puskesmas*. *Puskesmas* are supervised by doctors who provide maternal and child care, vaccinations, and disease control. Mobile *puskesmas* have been important in bringing free health care to many remote villages.

The poorest people in Indonesia get free health care. Many wealthier people in the country use its growing number of private clinics, while some travel to Singapore and Malaysia, where the private services are of higher quality.

CHANGING LIFESTYLE

Over the last 20 years or so, the lifestyles of Indonesians have changed. Fast foods appeared in their diet, and the country now has many fast food outlets. Smoking has become popular, and one out of four Indonesians smokes. Sedentary lifestyles are common in urban areas, where many people have office-based jobs and where there are few open spaces for exercising. All

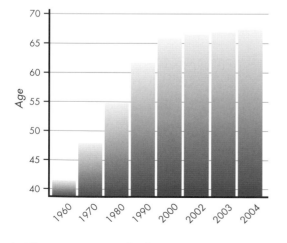

▲ Life expectancy at birth, 1960–2004

these changes are adversely affecting the health of millions of Indonesians. The amount of smoking-related respiratory and coronary illnesses is rising in the country. Traffic accidents also cause many deaths and injuries.

IMPROVING CHILD HEALTH

Although Indonesia's infant mortality rate fell to 31 deaths for every 1,000 live births in 2005, it is still double that of Malaysia. Diarrhea is a major killer. In recent years, cases of diarrhea have doubled among women and young children in the country. This illness is linked to poor sanitation and lack of basic health care.

Indonesia's level of poverty is rising, and this is causing more cases of malnutrition, especially among young children. One key sign of malnutrition is anemia, a low level of iron in the blood caused by a poor diet. More than 60 percent of children in Java are anemic. In some of the country's remote villages, there have been cases of marasmus. Marasmus is a disease that is commonly seen in malnourished children in Africa and is characterized by a bloated belly.

▶ The use of herbal remedies, called *jamu*, is common in Indonesia. These remedies come from roots, flowers, bark, nuts, herbs, and spices.

Focus on: Tuberculosis

More than half a million new cases of tuberculosis (TB) are reported in Indonesia each year, and 175,000 people die from this disease every year. Indonesia ranks third out of the 22 countries of the world with a high level of the disease. TB accounts for 7 percent of all diseases in the country, compared with just 4 percent in neighboring countries. A bacterial lung disease, TB can be treated with antibiotics, although the process is lengthy and expensive. The incidence of TB is often linked to HIV. In 2003, HIV infections leapt more than 60 percent to 210,000 new cases. Experts believe this rise is a result of the practice of reusing syringes in rural clinics.

CHAPTER 11

Culture and Religion

Indonesia has a rich culture of art and music based on many civilizations and religions. During the 1950s and 1960s, the arts in Indonesia were influenced by politics. One popular form of art was social realism, a style in which paintings reflected social issues. Djoko Pekik is well known for his paintings depicting the day-to-day problems of poor people in Indonesia. In 1966, many socialist artists in Indonesia were killed during the backlash against communists. Some went into exile while others, including writer Pramoedya Ananta Toer, were arrested. In place of social realist art, traditional art was encouraged, and artists with a modernist approach were discouraged. With the resignation of Suharto in 1998, artistic freedom was restored, and Indonesia's artists were free to explore all forms of art.

DANCE AND MUSIC

Dancing plays an important role in Indonesian culture, especially on the islands of Java and Bali, where dance and drama are combined. Traditional dance dramas are based on epic Hindu poems. The female dancers wear elaborate headdresses and colorful costumes. They also grow long nails to emphasize their hand movements. The dancing is usually accompanied by gamelan music. This type of music is played on percussion instruments, such as gongs, xylophones, and drums; flutes; and zithers.

Today, art and dance in Indonesia are influenced in many ways by the West. Modern choreographers blend Western styles with traditional Indonesian dance to reach a younger audience. The *sendratari,* for example, is a traditional dance drama in which the performers use modern costumes and movements. Indonesia is famous for its textiles and batik. Today, Indonesian artists are also experimenting with Western techniques. One example of this involves combining oil paints and batik.

◀ Dancers with elaborate headdresses take part in the Melasti ceremony in Denpasar, Bali, in 2005. This ceremony celebrates the victory of good over evil.

The country's most popular music is *dangdut*, which can be heard on the streets and in shops and bars. *Dangdut* is described as a modern dance rhythm influenced by rock, Indian film music, and urban Arab pop. One of the country's most famous *dangdut* singers is Rhoma Irama, who sings about Islam, social issues, and family values.

▲ Puppets such as these have been used in shadow theaters in Java for more than 1,000 years. The puppeteer manipulates the puppets so that their shadows move across a white screen.

Focus on: Pramoedya Ananta Toer

One of Indonesia's greatest authors is Pramoedya Ananta Toer, who was born in 1925. He was arrested and imprisoned three times because of his writing. Between 1947 and 1949, the Dutch held him because of his anticolonial views. For nine months in about 1955, the Sukarno government imprisoned him for publishing a book that was considered too sympathetic to the ethnic Chinese. Beginning in 1966, Toer was sent to the prison island of Buru for 14 years. While there, Toer told a story each night to his fellow prisoners to help them forget their suffering and hunger. After his release he published these stories in a set of four books called *Minke's Story*. These books are about a young Javanese boy living in Dutch colonial times. The first book, *This Earth of Mankind*, was published in 1981, and it became an instant bestseller. The Suharto government banned Toer's books, but pirated copies were widely read. In 2000, Toer was shortlisted for the Nobel Prize for Literature. He died in April 2006.

LANGUAGE

Bahasa Indonesia is the official language of Indonesia. It is a version of Malay that was commonly used throughout Indonesia by traders. It is a very simple language that has no verb tenses, noun genders, or articles. It is important because it is a language that unifies Indonesia. Bahasa is spoken mostly by people in urban areas. In the rural areas, people tend to speak the language associated with their ethnic group, and in East Timor, many people refuse to speak Bahasa. There are 580 other languages in use in Indonesia. Javanese, which originated on the island of Java, is spoken by about 45 percent of the population and 14 percent speak Sundanese. Some languages—such as Ruta and Soahuku, from Seram Island—are spoken only in a single village. Concern exists that some of these languages are spoken by so few people that one day they will be forgotten.

FOOD

The staple food of most Indonesians is rice. On some of the eastern islands, however, maize, sago, and root vegetables, such as cassava, taro, and sweet potatoes, are the staples. Coconut is found everywhere. Cooking oil is made from it, and its milk and flesh are used in many dishes.

Each province in Indonesia has its own style of cooking. Spices and hot chili peppers are used widely, especially in west Sumatra and north Sulawesi. Javanese recipes use vegetables, soybeans, beef, and chicken, while Sumatran dishes use more beef. Further to the east, fish—either grilled or curried—is a prominent ingredient. Pork is a speciality in Bali, Papua, and the highlands of northern Sumatra and northern Sulawesi.

? Did You Know?

Padang restaurants are everywhere in Indonesia. They serve hot, spicy dishes from Padang, which is located in western Sumatra. In these restaurants, the waiter brings dozens of small plates with various dishes to the table and the diners can eat whatever they like. At the end of the meal, they are charged just for the food that they have eaten.

◀ A traditional Indonesian meal consists of rice and a number of small meat or fish dishes.

 ▶ Indonesians celebrate Independence Day on August 17. This is one of several festival days celebrated in the country. Others include Idul Fitri, a festival celebrated by Muslims at the end of Ramadan.

RELIGION

The majority of Indonesians—87.2 percent—are Muslim. Indonesia has the largest population of Muslims in the world. The country's constitution guarantees freedom of religion, and people are allowed to follow the religion of their choice. More than 9 percent are Christians, most of whom are Protestant. Hinduism was once common in Indonesia, but now most Hindus are found on Bali and in eastern Java. Among Indonesia's Chinese minority, some are Buddhists, but there are also Christian and Muslim Chinese. Some Chinese are Confucians, but this was not a recognized faith in the country until recently. Some isolated communities in Indonesia are animist. Animists believe that animate and inanimate objects have a roh, or life-force, and practice ancestor and spirit worship.

In spite of the country's religious freedom, there has been conflict between its different religious groups. Since 1999, for example, clashes between Christians and Muslims on the Maluku Islands have claimed 6,000 lives. More fighting between religious groups has occurred in Poso in central Sulawesi.

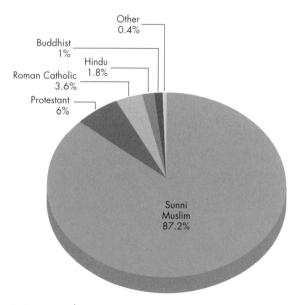

▲ Major religions

Other 0.4%
Buddhist 1%
Hindu 1.8%
Roman Catholic 3.6%
Protestant 6%
Sunni Muslim 87.2%

CHAPTER 12

Leisure and Tourism

Indonesians participate in a wide range of sports and leisure activities, both traditional and modern.

SPORTS FOR ALL

Indonesia's government is eager for people to participate in sports. National Sports Day is held each year on September 9. This day is considered to be important for unity because people from all over the country take part. The government sponsors a youth organization called Karang Taruna. A network of local leaders organizes activities, such as sports and community work, for members of Karang Taruna.

Among the most popular sports in Indonesia are badminton and tennis. The country's badminton players have dominated the sport internationally since the 1950s. When badminton became an Olympic sport at the 1992 Barcelona Olympics, Indonesia won all four gold medals. The country is successful internationally in other sports, too. For example, its tennis team has won many regional trophies, while its women's archery team won the country's first Olympic medal at the 1988 Olympics in Seoul, South Korea.

SOCCER

Young people in Indonesia play soccer, but they have to play on beaches or in parks with makeshift goals because there are few fields. Papuan villages have a communal ball that hangs in the goal net. People are allowed to play soccer as long as they replace the ball in the net afterward. The country has a national soccer league. To avoid too much expensive and difficult travel, its teams play a series of games in a region before returning home.

TRADITIONAL SPORTS

Traditional sports in Indonesia include boat racing; kite flying; *pencak silat*, a martial art similar to karate; and *sepak takraw*, or kick

▶ Most villages in Indonesia have a badminton court. All that is needed is a hard surface and a net. This court is in Bena village, on the island of Flores.

volleyball. *Sepak takraw* is a cross between soccer and volleyball that is played on a badminton court. It is played by two teams, each with three players and a substitute. The aim of the game is to keep a rattan ball in the air for as long as possible using any part of the body except the hands.

LEISURE TIME

Indonesians love watching films at movie theaters. All but the smallest villages have movie theaters. Foreign films with Bahasa Indonesia subtitles are shown in the larger cities such as Jakarta, Surabaya, and Denpasar. Many of Indonesia's larger cities lack recreational areas. In Jakarta, for example, land prices are high, and, in the past, governments have not put much land aside for recreation. One of the few open spaces is found around the national monument located near the city center. Each morning, thousands of people use this area for walking, jogging, cycling, aerobics, and tai chi (a Chinese system of movement for improving balance and health).

▲ These people have just taken part in a parade in which they dribbled soccer balls through the center of Jakarta. The purpose of this parade was to celebrate the 2002 World Cup final.

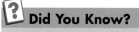 **Did You Know?**

Congklak is a popular family board game played on a wooden board with a series of small depressions along its sides. It uses 98 markers, usually shells or pebbles, that are placed in the depressions. The two players move the markers in a game of strategy and skill to reach the "home" depression.

TOURISM

Indonesia's long coastlines, palm-fringed beaches, and coral reefs make it a major tropical holiday destination. Most of the tourists visiting the country come from Singapore, Japan, Taiwan, Malaysia, Australia, Germany, and the United States. Annual revenue from tourism is worth about U.S.$5.2 billion.

Indonesia's vacation industry experienced setbacks as a result of the 2002 Bali bombing and the SARS epidemic in early 2003. Tourist numbers recovered slightly in 2004, when almost 5.5 million international tourists visited Indonesia. Numbers fell again following the tsunami in December 2004 and the Bali bombings of 2005. The Ministry of Culture and Tourism has tried to encourage tourism by inviting international tour operators to visit.

▼ The seas around Indonesia are home to about 15 percent of the world's coral reefs. The number of divers visiting these reefs is increasing each year. Java, Bali, Nusa Tanggara, and Sulawesi have well-known diving areas. The islands of Maluku, western Sumatra, and Papua have newer diving areas.

Indonesian embassies around the world have also been acting as unofficial tourism representatives by providing information about the country.

Tourism in Indonesia

- Tourist arrivals, millions: 5.3
- Earnings from tourism in U.S.$: 5,226,000,000
- Tourism as % foreign earnings: 5.8
- Tourist departures, millions: 2.076
- Expenditure on tourism in U.S.$: 4,570,000,000

Source: World Bank

BOROBODUR AND PRAMBANAN TEMPLES

Yogyakarta is one of Indonesia's main cultural centers because it lies close to the huge Borobodur (Buddhist) and Prambanan (Hindu) temples, which are both World Heritage sites. Borobodur was built between A.D. 778 and 850. Within one hundred years the temple was

buried beneath a mountain of volcanic ash from Mount Merapi. It remained buried until 1814, when it was rediscovered by Sir Thomas Stamford Raffles. The temple was cleared of ash, but it was damaged, so a major restoration project was started with help from UNESCO in 1975. The temple was finally opened to the public in 1983. The Prambanan temple complex dates from the tenth century and contains temples dedicated to the Hindu gods Shiva, Vishnu, and Brahma.

BEACHES AND VOLCANOES

Bali has long been a popular destination and is considered to be the "jewel in the crown" of Indonesia's tourist industry. It has beautiful beaches and temples and picturesque rice terraces. The recent bombings in Bali, however, have caused some tourists to stay away. Now, the islands lying to the east of Bali, known as Nusa Tanggara, are attracting more visitors, especially the island of Lombok. These islands are well known as a top surfing destination. Another attraction is the large reptile, the Komodo dragon, which is found only on the island of Komodo. Some of Java's biggest natural attractions are its volcanoes, especially Mount Bromo. A popular tourist activity is a climb to the summit of Mount Bromo to see the sunrise.

ECOTOURISM

Indonesia's government is trying to encourage ecotourism, especially in the country's rain forest and coral reef areas. Ecotourism holidays allow people to get close to nature. For example, ecotourists in Indonesia can watch orangutans in the rain forest or help with turtle conservation projects in Sulawesi. Ecotourism puts money back into Indonesia's communities and helps to provide employment in some of the country's more remote areas.

▼ The Komodo dragon is found only on the island of Komodo. This huge reptile can be very dangerous so the tourists are staying a safe distance behind it.

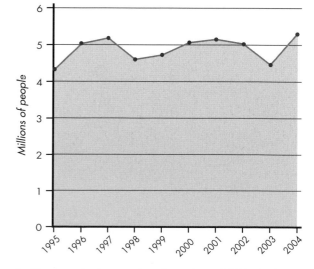

▲ Changes in international tourism, 1995–2004

CHAPTER 13

Environment and Conservation

Since Indonesia's independence, the country's governments have focused on economic growth and paid little attention to the environment. Over the years, the country has suffered widespread environmental damage. Problems include air and water pollution in Java and deforestation across Indonesia.

AIR POLLUTION

The large number of poorly maintained vehicles and the use of cheap, poor quality fuels mean that the air quality in most of Indonesia's cities is very poor. The high level of small particles from exhaust in the air causes breathing difficulties, particularly among the elderly and those suffering from heart conditions. Jakarta is the third most polluted city in the world, after Mexico City and Bangkok. Its air quality is not improving. In 2005, Jakarta experienced only 20 days of fresh air, compared to 21 days in 2003 and 25 days in 2002. In 2005, new laws were passed to control vehicle emissions and to require all public vehicles to run on LPG (liquefied petroleum gas) in an attempt to improve air quality.

THE THREAT FROM LEAD

The World Bank has identified exposure to lead as the greatest environmental threat to the health of Indonesians, especially children. Lead is found in the emissions of lead smelters and vehicles running on leaded fuels, as well as in lead paints. Children are very sensitive to lead and it can adversely affect their behavior and mental development. Indonesia's government started to phase out leaded fuels in 2001.

Hazardous waste from industry is an increasing problem in Indonesia. The country has few controls over its disposal, which means that much of the waste ends up in dumps in urban areas. Hazardous waste from other countries, such as computers for recycling, also ends up in Indonesia. Companies in countries, such as the United States, the Netherlands, Singapore, and

◀ Traffic jams during the morning rush hour are common in Jakarta and emit a lot of pollution.

► New roads are cleared through the rain forests of Kalimantan in order to bring in heavy machinery and take out logs. The new roads open up more areas of forest for exploitation.

Japan find it cheaper to send their waste to Indonesia than to dispose of it at home. Some of this waste has been placed in landfill sites where the hazardous materials contaminate groundwater. The effects of this pollution may be felt for many decades.

DEFORESTATION

In 1988, Dr. Norman Myers, a leading ecologist, described Indonesia's rain forests as a biodiversity hotspot because of the vast numbers of plants and animals that live in them. These valuable forests are being cleared at a frightening rate. Between 1990 and 2005, more than one-quarter of the country's forests were cleared.

There are several reasons for the clearing of forests in Indonesia. Trees are felled for their valuable hardwood, for veneers, and for plywood to export. They are cleared for mining, oil palm plantations, rubber plantations, and to supply wood pulp to the huge pulp and paper industry. Unlike many other countries of the world, Indonesia's pulp and paper industry has not replanted forests; it has simply cleared more primary forest. Land

in Indonesia is also cleared to make space for migrant families. In addition, illegal logging contributes to deforestation.

The continuing loss of forest and the abuse of the rights and customs of the indigenous peoples who live in them has caused outrage around the world. Considerable international pressure has been put on Indonesia's government to take action. In 2005, Indonesia started to develop a strategy to manage the country's forests sustainably and to stamp out illegal logging.

? Did You Know?

In 1997, huge forest fires caused by deforestation and drought spread across Kalimantan and Sumatra. The smoke from these fires increased air pollution levels across Southeast Asia, and the pollution reached as far as Australia and Thailand. On September 23, 1997, the air pollution index hit a record 839 micrograms per cubic meter ($\mu g/m3$) in Sarawak, Malaysia. The air pollution index is a measure of the mass of tiny particles of solid matter in the air from fires and vehicle exhausts; usually, levels are well below 100. Levels of more than 300 are considered to be hazardous to health.

CONSERVATION

Of the 2,467 or so known species of amphibians, birds, mammals, and reptiles found in Indonesia, about 30 percent are endemic. That is, they are found in no other country; they are unique to Indonesia. This rich biodiversity makes it vitally important for Indonesia's habitats to be protected through various conservation programs.

The country's first national park—Ujung Kulon National Park, in Java—was established by the Dutch in 1921 to protect the endangered Javan rhinoceros. Today, there are 50 rhinos, and their population is stable. Patrols in the park and along the coast help prevent poachers from reaching the rhinos. Other endangered species in the park include the Javan gibbon (a small ape) and the banteng, a type of wild cow.

Another protected area in Indonesia is Bukit Barisan Selatan, on Sumatra. It is a rain-forest area surrounded by villages and farmland. In this shrinking reserve, there are 300 species of birds, as well as Sumatran rhinos, tigers, elephants, sun bears, bearded pigs, tapirs, gibbons, rare orchids, and rafflesia plants.

Other protected areas in the country include Lorentz National Park in Papua, covering about 6.2 million acres (2.5 million hectares); Komodo National Park, which protects the Komodo dragons; and the Leuser Ecosystem, in Aceh. The Leuser Ecosystem is a huge forested area. It is believed to be the last remaining place where elephants, rhinos, tigers, clouded leopards, and orangutans can all be found living together.

Environmental and Conservation Data

📂 Forested area as % total land area: 59.7

📂 Protected area as % total land area: 12.5

📂 Number of protected areas: 965

SPECIES DIVERSITY

Category	Known species	Threatened species
Mammals	515	147
Breeding birds	929	114
Reptiles	745	28
Amphibians	278	n/a
Fish	4,080	68
Plants	29,375	384

Source: World Resources Institute

◀ A young boy hunts for bits of plastic floating among the garbage in a polluted river in Jakarta in 2006. He will be able to sell the plastic to earn some money.

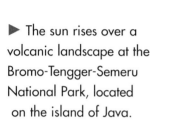
► The sun rises over a volcanic landscape at the Bromo-Tengger-Semeru National Park, located on the island of Java.

THREATS TO THE REEFS

Indonesia's coral reefs are among the most biologically rich reefs in the world, with about 1,600 species of fish and 480 species of coral. About half of them, however, are facing a medium-to-high risk of damage. Healthy reefs are important. Not only do they support the fisheries, but they also act as breakwaters to protect the coast from storm surges. The reefs are threatened by overfishing and industrial wastes, fertilizers, pesticides, and sewage. Silt makes the water cloudy, blocking the sunlight that corals need in order to grow. The soil erosion that follows deforestation increases the amount of silt carried by the rivers.

In 1998, the World Bank provided U.S.$7 million for the Coral Reef Rehabilitation and Management Program to promote sustainable environmental development. Pilot projects were set up in Taka Bone Rate National Park, in south Sulawesi, and Lease Islands, in Maluku. The program has succeeded best when communities have been allowed to manage their local reefs and where "no-take" zones have been established to create sanctuaries for fish.

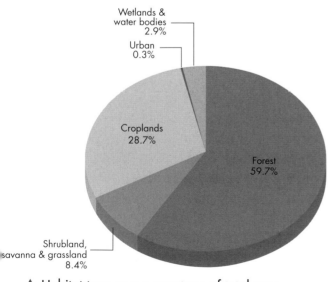

Wetlands & water bodies 2.9%
Urban 0.3%
Croplands 28.7%
Forest 59.7%
Shrubland, savanna & grassland 8.4%

▲ Habitat type as a percentage of total area

Focus on: The Green Coast Project

After the tsunami of 2004, conservation organizations led by Wetlands International, IUCN, and WWF set up the Green Coast Project. The aim of the project is to restore coastal ecosystems such as mangrove swamps in the tsunami-hit Asian countries. This project will provide the coastal communities of Sumatra with new fisheries and natural protection from storms, cyclones, and future tsunamis.

CHAPTER 14

Future Challenges

Following his election in 2004, President Yudhoyono said he was committed to encouraging economic growth, creating jobs, and beating poverty. Other issues facing Indonesia include combating illegal logging, fighting corruption, preventing terrorism, and rebuilding the areas of Aceh and Nias damaged by the 2004 tsunami and the 2005 earthquake.

▼ Fishing is an important industry in Aceh. Aid programs are financing the replacing of boats and nets destroyed by the 2004 tsunami.

ECONOMIC PROBLEMS

In 2004, fuel subsidies cost the country as much as U.S.$8 billion and meant that less money was available to fund social services and development projects. The abolition of the subsidies in the fall of 2005 meant that the government could start investing in services such as health care, education, water, and sanitation. But the government was soon faced with economic problems. The rise in fuel prices caused inflation, and since 2005, many businesses have gone bankrupt and many people have lost their jobs. It is likely that growth will be slower in the short term, while businesses and the public adjust to the higher fuel costs. In the long term, Indonesia's government must allow for lower production from its own oil and gas fields and increase the amount of electricity that is generated using renewable energy sources.

Various events have influenced Indonesia's economy. Although the tsunami in Aceh and the earthquake in Nias did not have a huge effect on the national economy (less than 0.5 percent of GDP), the damage to these areas was severe. In Aceh, the cost of the damage was estimated at U.S.$4.5 billion, although many of the costs of rebuilding will by paid by international donors. It will take many years for the economies of these regions to recover.

Terrorist incidents in 2005 reduced the number of tourists visiting the country. This especially affected Bali, where the tourist industry had just recovered from the 2002 bombing. In late 2005, Indonesia reported 16 cases of human avian influenza, or bird flu. These reports sparked panic, and, again, tourists stayed away.

► Mangrove swamps help to protect coasts from tidal surges. These workers in Aceh are potting mangrove saplings that will be used to restore damaged mangrove swamps along the coast.

ILLEGAL LOGGING

There is no doubt that illegal logging is one of the most pressing issues facing Indonesia. In spite of the tough government statements and new policies to fight illegal logging, illegal logging is increasing. Regional self-rule is at the root of the problem, because each province manages its own forests and issues logging concessions. Existing laws are ineffective in stopping the activities of corrupt officials, many of whom work with powerful figures in organized crime. Some experts have warned that, if current rates of logging continue, no forest will be left in Indonesia outside of the national parks in fewer than 15 to 20 years.

Indonesia has huge natural resources in the form of hardwood forests, rich agricultural soils, oil and gas reserves, and valuable metals, such as copper, gold, and tin. If the government can achieve its aims of eradicating corruption, reducing poverty, and creating jobs—and succeed in pulling the country's many different peoples together—Indonesia has the potential to become one of the richest countries in the world.

? Did You Know?

Indonesia's government selected seven priority areas for 2006. They were:
1. Reducing poverty
2. Creating jobs and increasing investment and exports
3. Revitalizing agriculture and rural areas
4. Improving accessibility and quality of education and health care
5. Improving law enforcement, eradicating corruption, and reforming bureaucracy
6. Improving security and defenses
7. Reconstructing Aceh and Nias

Time Line

c. 850 The Buddhist temple of Borobodur on the island of Java is completed.

1292 Explorer Marco Polo lands in Sumatra.

1511 Portuguese traders reach Indonesia.

1596 Dutch traders claim West Timor.

1623 The Dutch East India Company takes control of Indonesia.

1799 The Dutch East India Company closes down. Control of Indonesia passes to the Dutch government.

1815 Mount Tambora, on Sumbawa Island, erupts, killing about 50,000 people and sending a cloud of volcanic dust around the world.

1883 The volcano Krakatoa erupts, creating a 130-foot (40-m) tsunami in Indonesia's Sunda Strait and killing 36,000 people in Java and Sumatra.

1918 The Dutch set up the Volksraad in Jakarta.

1927 The Indonesian Nationalist Party is formed.

1942 Japan invades the Dutch East Indies, and the Dutch colonial government surrenders to Japan.

1945 Japan's army surrenders, and Sukarno and Hatta declare independence for Indonesia. Indonesian nationalists spend the next four years fighting Dutch troops. East Timor remains under Portuguese control.

1949 Indonesia gains independence and Sukarno becomes president.

1965 Six army officers are assassinated, causing rioting in the streets. Mass arrests of communists take place, and as many as 500,000 Chinese Indonesians are killed.

1966 Sukarno gives Suherto the authority to bring the country to order.

1967 Suharto becomes president.

1969 West Papua becomes a province of Indonesia and is renamed Irian Jaya.

1975 Portugal grants independence to East Timor, but Indonesia annexes it. In the following months, 600,000 people are killed.

1994 Mount Merapi, an active volcano in central Java, erupts violently, killing 43 people.

1997 The value of Indonesia's currency falls during the Asian Currency Crisis, and resulting in demonstrations in the country's streets.

1998 Suharto resigns, and B.J. Habibie becomes president.

1999 Abdurrahman Wahid is elected as Indonesia's new president. East Timor votes for independence in a United Nations-sponsored referendum. Anti-independence militia kill thousands of people, and UN peacekeeping troops move into East Timor.

2001 Ethnic violence takes place in Kalimantan, where indigenous Dayaks force out Madurese migrants. Megawati Sukarnoputri is elected president.

2002 East Timor becomes independent. Irian Jaya is renamed Papua. (October 12) A car bomb explodes outside a nightclub in Bali, killing 200 people and injuring 300 others, the worst terrorist act in Indonesia's history.

2003 (August 5) A car bomb explodes outside the Marriott Hotel in Jakarta, killing 10 people and wounding 149, including two Americans.

2004 Susilo Bambang Yudhoyono becomes president in Indonesia's first direct presidential election.

2004 (December 26) A powerful undersea earthquake off the coast of Sumatra creates a huge tsunami that floods coasts and kills about 130,000 people in Indonesia.

2005 (March 28) A major earthquake hits the west coast of northern Sumatra; more than 1,300 people die, most of them on the island of Nias.

2005 (August 15) Indonesia's government and Aceh rebels sign a peace treaty in Helsinki to end the nearly 30 years of fighting, during which 15,000 people were killed. (October 1) Three bombs explode in Bali, killing 23 people, including the bombers.

2006 (May 27) An earthquake occurs on the island of Java, hitting the city of Yogyakarta and killing more than 6,000 people. (July) A second earthquake occurs off the coast of Java; it is followed by a 9.8-foot (3-m) tsunami that kills 650 people. (December) The former spokesperson for the Free Aceh Movement, Irwandi Yusuf, wins the first direct election for governor of the province of Aceh.

Glossary

Allies the groups of countries that fought against Germany and Japan in World War II, including Britain, the United States, Canada, and Australia

archipelago a group of islands

authoritarianism a style of government in which the leader is not appointed in free elections and the people are subjected to strict controls and restricted freedom

bribery offering or giving something of value (usually money) to influence the action of an official

colonial relating to people settling in a different country from their own and applying their laws and language to that country

Confucians followers of the teachings of Confucius, a Chinese philosopher who lived from 551–479 B.C.

decentralize to distribute responsibility from central to regional government

ethnic group people of the same cultural, racial, or religious origins

genocide the deliberate destruction of an entire people or ethnic group

Gross Domestic Product (GDP) the total value of goods and services produced within the borders of a country

indigenous coming from a particular area

International Court of Justice a court set up to settle disputes between members of the United Nations

International Monetary Fund (IMF) an organization that oversees monetary cooperation between nations and lends money to countries that are experiencing financial difficulties

International Union for the Conservation of Nature and Natural Resources (IUCN) a worldwide conservation network

literate able to read and write

mangrove a type of tropical tree that grows in forests in swampy areas along coasts of tropical oceans

marasmus an extreme form of malnutrition caused by lack of protein and energy foods in the diet

militia a military group made up of members of the general population to assist the army in an emergency, or a rebel group opposing the regular army

net importer a country that imports more of something than it exports

organized crime crime carried out by groups of people who organized for the purpose of illegally making money or influencing politics

plywood a sheet of wood made up of three or more thin sheets of wood bonded together with glue

realism a style of art in which the subject matter is shown as accurately and realistically as possible

referendum a vote among a group of people on a single issue

rickshaw a small, two-wheeled cart pulled by one person

SARS Severe Acute Respiratory Syndrome; a respiratory disease that first appeared in China in 2003

separatists people who want to break away from a group, for example, to form a separate country

Sharia traditional Islamic law based on the Koran and the teachings of the Prophet Muhammad

socialist a person who favors socialism, an economic system based in theory on public ownership and the equal distribution of wealth

sustainable capable of being maintained or repeated

United Nations (UN) an international organization formed in 1945 to promote peace, security, and economic development

World Bank the sister organization of the IMF that lends money to countries when no other funds are available

WWF an independent, global conservation organization that works in more than 90 countries

Further Information

BOOKS TO READ

Burton, Tristan. *Indonesia*
(Countries of the World).
Facts on File, 2005.

Cramer, Mark and Frederick Fisher.
Indonesia (Countries of the World).
Gareth Stevens, 2000.

Miller, Debra A. *Indonesia*
(Modern Nations of the World).
Lucent Books, 2005.

Phillips, Douglas A. *Indonesia*
(Modern World Nations) Chelsea
House Publications, 2004.

Townsend, John. *The Asian Tsunami 2004*
(When Disaster Struck) Raintree, 2006.

Zuehlke, Jeffrey. *Indonesia in Pictures*
(Visual Geography). Twenty-first
Century Books, 2005.

USEFUL WEB SITES

CIA World Factbook: Indonesia
www.cia.gov/cia/publications/factbook/
geos/id.html

Indonesian Gamelan
www.seasite.niu.edu/indonesian/budaya_
bangsa/Gamelan/Main_Page/main_page.htm

PBS: Wild Indonesia
www.pbs.org/wildindonesia

Time: Asia's Tsunami
www.time.com/time/asia/photoessays/tsunami/
indonesia5.html

Time: Bali Confessions
www.time.com/time/asia/covers/501030127/

BBC News: Unravelling Krakatoa's Secrets
news.bbc.co.uk/1/hi/sci/tech/4972522.stm

Publisher's note to educators and parents: Our editors have
carefully reviewed these Web sites to ensure that they are
suitable for children. Many Web sites change frequently,
however, and we cannot guarantee that a site's future
contents will continue to meet our high standards of quality
and educational value. Be advised that children should
be closely supervised whenever they access the Internet.

Index

Page numbers in **bold** indicate pictures.

About the Author

Sally Morgan is an experienced author of children's books and has written on a wide range of topics, including nature, science, geography, and environmental issues. She is particularly interested in wildlife and conservation and has traveled to Southeast Asia on many occasions to photograph rain-forest wildlife.